John Courtenay

Philosophical Reflections on the Late Revolution in France,

And the Conduct of the Dissenters in England, in a Letter to the Rev. Dr.

Priestley. Second Edotion

John Courtenay

Philosophical Reflections on the Late Revolution in France,
And the Conduct of the Dissenters in England, in a Letter to the Rev. Dr. Priestley.
Second Edotion

ISBN/EAN: 9783744716406

Printed in Europe, USA, Canada, Australia, Japan

Cover: Foto ©Thomas Meinert / pixelio.de

More available books at **www.hansebooks.com**

PHILOSOPHICAL REFLECTIONS

ON THE LATE

REVOLUTION IN FRANCE, &c.

PHILOSOPHICAL REFLECTIONS

ON THE LATE

REVOLUTION IN FRANCE,

AND THE CONDUCT OF

THE DISSENTERS IN ENGLAND;

IN A LETTER TO

THE REV. DR. PRIESTLEY,

BY J. COURTENAY, ESQ. M.P.

QUO, QUO SCELESTI RUITIS?———HOR.

THE SECOND EDITION WITH ADDITIONS,

LONDON:
PRINTED FOR T. BECKET, PALL-MALL.
MDCCXC.

PHILOSOPHICAL REFLECTIONS

ON THE LATE

REVOLUTION IN FRANCE, &c.

ADDRESSED TO

THE REV. DR. PRIESTLEY.

S I R,

I AM not in the leaft furprifed that fome of
the moft enlightened men of the prefent
age, equally diftinguifhed by genius, fcience,
and tafte, are ferioufly alarmed at the dangerous and rapid progrefs of democracy in
France. We had indeed little to fear, whilft
they enjoyed that ferene and tranquil ftate
of government, uniformly refulting from the
unlimited power of a monarch, and the feu-

B   dal

dal privileges of a numerous, polifhed, and gallant *noblefſe*. Whilſt the various orders of a pious, rich, and fplendid hierarchy anxiouſly watched over the temporal and eternal concerns of a docile obſequious laity, preaching up the catholic apoſtolic doctrine of paſſive obedience and non-reſiſtance,— internal peace, ſubordination, and ſubmiſ-ſion, were the characteriſtics of that gay, volatile, and ingenious people.—But now, *horreſco referens*, they no longer acknow-ledge " The right divine of kings to go-" vern wrong;" and inſtead of bending their necks to the vice-gerent of heaven, prefumptuouſly look into the ſacred ark, queſtion the conduct of the Lord's anointed, and on abſtract metaphyſical principles (un-happily reduced into practice) aſſert the un-alienable right of man to freedom :—The fatal conſequences are obvious; as it is a political truth, confirmed by the experience of ages, that the tranquillity and happineſs

of

of a well regulated community can only be maintained by implicit obedience and unconditional fubmiffion. The vifions of chimerical fpeculation muft difappear before the light of hiftory, and truth and reafon again refume their empire over the human mind. I fay then, if the Athenians had quietly and judicioufly fubmitted to the dominion of the thirty tyrants, Critias, and his council of *ariftocrates* would not have been compelled to ftain their hands in the blood of their fellow-citizens. Socrates might have faved himfelf and his country, if he had exerted his abilities, like Doctor H. by fupporting the civil and ecclefiaftical eftablifhment of Athens, inftead of proudly and obftinately difplaying that factious and heterodox fpirit which has always diftinguifhed you. If Brutus, and his band of Roman confpirators, had faluted Julius Cæfar, king, defpotifm and felicity would have been diffufed over the world,

and

and an Englifh prelate *(a)* would not have difgraced himfelf, and his holy function, by pronouncing an eulogium on affaffination, and recommending the dangerous and daring tenets of a heathenifh ballad to our ingenuous youth, in the infidious and captivating language of claffical eloquence.—But let me, in the words of Lord Bacon, bring this topic home to men's bufinefs and bofoms. If Mr. Hampden had meekly acquiefced in Charles's claim to fhip-money, the nation would have been preferved from the horrors of a civil war ; " taxation, " no tyranny," would have become our political creed ;—America might ftill have flourifhed under our aufpices;—the uncontaminated loyalty of toryifm would have been our own ;—we fhould not have incurred the wrath of Heaven for fhedding the royal martyr's blood ; we fhould not have been punifhed for that flagitious act by the Revolution !—nor have had a Prince

of

of the Houfe of Brunfwick *to fuffer for our fins:*—We might ftill have enjoyed a Popifh liturgy *(b)*, a Calviniftical creed *(c)*, and an Arminian clergy *(d)*, with all the fuper-added bleffings of an arbitrary monarchy.

The populous and flourifhing kingdom of Dahomey on the gold coaft of Africa, is another ftriking example of the invaluable benefits of abfolute power. The king is there a king indeed, being the abfolute mafter of the lives and fortunes of his fubjects! *(e)* " They are," we are told, " a happy people, " and have a great contempt for the fubjects " of the neighbouring republics." A fimilar fentiment is thus beautifully expreffed by a Tory poet:—

" Still to ourfelves in every place confign'd,
" Our own felicity we make or find ;—
" The lifted ax, the agonizing wheel,
" Luke's iron crown, and Damien's bed of fteel,
" To men remote from power, but rarely known,
" Leave reafon, faith, and confcience all our own."

THE TRAVELLER.

I flatter

I flatter myfelf, that I have already proved to your fatisfaction, by examples taken both from ancient and modern hiftory, and from recent facts—elucidated by moral reafoning, that the vicious and oppreffive conduct of our rulers can only be effectually checked and counteracted by patience, humility, and long fuffering; and that all our political evils folely originate from tumult, infurrection, and rebellion. Let us learn a leffon of wifdom from the untutored favages of Dahomey;—they preferve their lives and property from royal rapacity and violence, by a cheerful refignation of both to the nod of their fovereign. A grave divine earneftly recommends the fame fyftem of quietifm to the fair fex, as an effectual prefervative againft any poffible violation of their chaftity *(f)*.

I fhall now proceed in demonftrating, that the Chriftian religion is to all intents and purpofes abolifhed in France; and that
the

the National Affembly have covertly and infidioufly introduced a fyftem of atheifm in its ftead. The fenate of *democrates* have commenced their impious fcheme by abolifhing tythes; a provifion appropriated and fanctified, *jure divino,* for the comfortable fupport of the clergy, by Heathens, Jews, and Chriftians *(g).* They have facrilegioufly prefumed to feize on the ancient revenue of the church, under the impious pretext of public good; of encouraging agriculture, by eafing the peafants of an unequal and oppreffive ecclefiaftical *corvée;* and of providing a better and more fuitable maintenance for the fecular and parochial priefts, who *alone* perform the refpective duties of their function. Thus have the National Affembly reduced atheifm into a fyftem, by feizing on the lands of the clergy, with an avowed defign of either pledging them as a fecurity for the national debt, or felling them to Turks, Jews, and Infidels,

for

for the difcharge of it. Befides, if bifhops, archbifhops, *abbés*, and the fuperior and dignified ranks of the hierarchy, are deprived of riches, immunities, power, and grandeur, how can they fhew their contempt of them? You invidioufly fnatch from thefe *Senecas*, thefe Chriftian ftoics, the fublime merit of optional virtue, by compelling them to practice temperance and moderation, not from choice, but neceffity.

A fimilar facrilegious attempt to abolifh tythes in Ireland, is a melancholy proof of the turbulent and innovating fpirit of the prefent times. The depreffed ftate of the clergy too evidently appears by the ftyle of their writings. Their arguments are fingly founded on the impolicy and injuftice of depriving them of a provifion fanctioned by antiquity, and folemnly entailed on them by the laws of the land. They have given up the vantage ground on which they ftood, ftript themfelves, of the celeftial armour,

the

the panoply divine, with which they were clad, and have rafhly ventured into the field naked and unarmed.

They have fucceeded accordingly.—If the clergy once weakly admit the profane interference of parliament; if they once admit, that this provifion may be modified, and even abolifhed by the fame authority;— if the conteft is merely to reft on the fallacious deductions of human reafon, it would indeed be difficult for the church to maintain the argument. Even the fpecious ftatement of the celebrated author of *The Wealth of Nations* (b) has little weight with me; for granting that tythes are often a fifth, and even a fourth, inftead of a tenth; though they are a check to induftry, &c. ftill the more unequal and more oppreffive this facred burthen may be, the more meritorious it is in thofe who fubmit to it from a confcientious motive, without murmuring and repining. A leading member of the Irifh

Houfe

House of Commons * has expatiated in his usual style of energetick, but delusive eloquence, on the great advantage which the church would derive from an Act of Commutation.—Law-suits, bickerings, and animosities, he asserted, would cease at once; and the mild spirit of peace and Christian charity, would mutually endear the pastor and his flock to each other. The clergy, no doubt, are perfectly sensible of this; and only persist in claiming tythes, as being their exclusive property by divine institution; and thinking that by accepting any commutation, however beneficial, they would betray the cause of God and religion.

And now, Sir, permit me to address you, in the most serious manner, on the most serious subject. What can democratick frenzy alledge against episcopacy? Were not bishops instituted by the apostles themselves, to enlighten and govern the

* Mr. Grattan.

primitive

primitive church? Though they foon difplayed an exterior pomp and fplendour in
their veftments, and in the celebration of
divine worfhip; though they affumed impe-
rial grandeur, inhabited palaces, afcended
their thrones; though they cenfured, con-
trolled, and excommunicated emperors; yet
they only fubmitted to this pageantry, and
reluctantly exercifed this temporal power,
merely to imprefs the congregation of the
faithful with a holy awe and veneration for
the MAJESTY of the church; well knowing
that found morality and the focial duties
could reft fecurely on no other bafis. Dr.
Mofheim's mifreprefentation on this very
interefting point, is defervedly treated with
contempt (i).—That bold and infidious
writer, under the fpecious pretext of candour and moderation, infpires his readers
with an averfion to all ecclefiaftical power,
and with indignation againft the clergy, for
having invariably fomented religious con-

troverfy

troverfy on myfterious unintelligible tenets; for encouraging perfecution, and pro-
moting the mifery of mankind in this
world, by infufing into their minds a
fpirit of hatred, malice, and uncharitable-
nefs; which at laft became the theological
characteriftick of every various difcordant
fect of Chriftianity. But if this ecclefiaftical hiftorian had been candid, (even
allowing the fact,) he fhould have fairly
acknowledged that the unrelenting virulence and embittered rancour of perfecution are the moft infallible criterions of
true belief, and the beft proof of a fervent
and fincere zeal for religion. As each fect
ftigmatized its antagonift by the odious de-
nomination of heretick,—Arians and Atha-
nafians, mutually actuated by the pureft mo-
tives of brotherly love and affection, in-
flicted a momentary and tranfient punifhment on the bodies of each other, either
by the fword or the ftake; left by conti-
nuing

nuing too long in their refpective fchifmatick opinions, they might forfeit all hope of falvation.

Thus the fame actions, erroneoufly confidered on mere abftract notions of philanthropy, may well appear unjuft, cruel, and barbarous; but their very effence is changed when viewed through this juft theological medium; for the genuine and beneficent fpirit of orthodoxy confecrates the apparent inhumanity of the action, by fanctifying the motive.

A century ago, an attempt to violate the fhred of a prieft's garment would have been deemed the higheft impiety;—but that happy period is long paft. A new fect of philofophers has brought all the prefent calamities on France, by infidioufly varying and adapting their writings to the tafte, and comprehenfion, of all ranks of fociety. They have perverted their underftandings, and corrupted their morals, by fatally per-
fuading

fuading them that juftice and benevolence were the effential duties of man, and that without bewildering themfelves in the teaz⁻ ing perplexities and inextricable myfteries of theology, they fhould " look through nature up to nature's God *(k)*." They have rent the facred veil afunder, and falfe⁻ ly and prefumptuoufly *taught*, that all power originates from the people;—that. kings are only the firft magiftrates of the ftate, and indebted to the loweft peafants for the fplendour, magnificence, and majefty that furround them; and that the greateft and meaneft fubject fhould be equally bound, and equally protected by the laws. Under the fpecious pretext of checking and expofing fuperftition and bigotry, they have profanely maintained, that the ordination of the prieft does not alter the nature of the man; and that the fole utility of his function confifts in inftructing the people in the moral and focial duties of life. They have calumniated the

ambaffadors

ambassadors of Heaven, by charging them
with having monopolised a third of the
landed revenue of the kingdom, by artfully
working on the confciences of the weak
and credulous, and extorting from them on
the bed of ficknefs, and even at the hour
of death, a fhare of their property, as a
propitiation for their fins. Their avowed
principles, fay thefe apoftles of impiety,
their uniform practice, the very fpirit of
their profeffion, mark them as implacable
enemies to fcience, philofophy, and intellectual liberty. A conftellation of genius
feemed united in propagating thefe dangerous atheiftical tenets. They were diffufed
in every fpecies of writing, and the dulcet
poifon was greedily imbibed in every part
of Europe. The moft poignant ridicule,
the fineft fallies of wit, the moft brilliant
traits of imagination, threw a falfe luftre
over this deceptious fyftem. The pernicious dogmas of their fchool, captivated the

2   attention,

attention, and were conveyed to the heart in the enchanting page of a novel, amidſt the feigned adventures and paſſionate endearments of lovers. An article of faith was expoſed in an epigram; ſcepticiſm allured proſelytes by a *bon mot*; and creeds were confuted in a ſong. The luminous ſcrutiniſing genius of Monteſquieu; the ſplendid levity of Voltaire; the impaſſioned and faſcinating eloquence of Rouſſeau; the preciſion and depth of d'Alembert; the bold and acute inveſtigations of Boulanger; the daring paradoxical ſpirit of Helvetius; the majeſtick ſublimity of the ſyſtematick Buffon; the profound aſtronomical reſearches of Bailly; the captivating elegance of Marmontel; the impreſſive condenſed thoughts of Diderot;—all theſe with combined force aſſailed and unſettled the conſecrated opinions of ages. The venerable Gothick ſtructure was ſhaken from its very foundation; the ſacred edifice is now laid low, and the

madneſs

fnadnefs of democracy has vainly dedicated a temple to liberty on its ruins.

And are we not at this inftant menaced with fimilar calamities, by a dangerous combination of fanatical literati? Have not our prophetical Elijahs obferved a cloud in the eaft, pregnant with inflammatory particles, and juft ready to burft on this devoted land?—But to drop the metaphor. Has not a *catechifm (l)* gone forth, teaching us, that churches are houfes built of wood and ftone, which do not change their nature, though rendered holy by thofe fanctimonious ceremonies which the hierarchy have ordained? Are we not told, that neither *(m)* epifcopacy nor tythes are of apoftolick inftitution; that bifhops are not chofen by the *people*, but appointed by the mockery of a royal *congé d'elire?*— Are we not alfo told, that the primitive church confifted folely of the people, their leaders, and the *minifters* or *deacons?* Can

D   you,

you, Sir, then, have the effrontery to deny that the exalted character of the lords fpiritual is depreciated, and their facred authority contemptuoufly treated, in this abominable catechifm; Is it not recommended by a plotting and dangerous fynod, confifting of four or five hundred turbulent heretical non-conformifts, who proudly denominate themfelves the Eaftern Affociation? Their enthufiaftick zeal makes them truly formidable; their fame has gone forth into all lands. Their miffionaries have excited tumults and infurrections at Tibet and Conftantinople; for they deteft every mode of ecclefiaftical jurifdiction, and equally hate the *Mufti*, the grand *Lama*, and the Archbifhop of Canterbury. Have not thefe catechumenical lectures been tranflated into all languages? Has not the prefent emperor of China iffued an edict to have them feized and burnt, with every mark of ignominy, as

containing

containing feditious and irreligious doctrines, highly injurious to the rational
and moral precepts of Confucius? The
great inquifitorial council of Japan have
proceeded with their ufual vindictive
impetuofity, and have actually impaled
fix of thofe mifchievous zealots, who
were difpatched by the Eaftern Affociation, at an enormous expence, to dif-
perfe this alarming tract through every nation and country under Heaven! Nay, fo
inveterate is the malignancy cf this fynod,
that they have lately made up this catechifm into a fpecifick, which, agreeable to
their accuftomed cant, they call *fpiritual re-
generating* pills. Thefe are prefcribed to be
taken by nurfes, and women during a ftate
of pregnancy; that children at the breaft
may fuck in thefe curfed doctrines with
their milk, the embrio ideas of infants
be contaminated before they are born, and
a new ftimulative be added to original fin.

By

By this diabolical invention, faction, rebellion, and anarchy, may be diffeminated over
the globe, and the flourishing empires of
China and Japan be overturned by a future
generation * of Arians, Socinians, Pela-
geans, Neceffarians, Antinomians, and Ma-
terialifts !

" *The babe, ere yet he draws his vital breath,*
" Receives the lurking principle of death ;
" The young difeafe, that muft fubdue at length,
" Grows with his growth, and ftrengthens with his
     ftrength."

If fome vigorous and coercive meafures
are not adopted to check thefe audacious
proceedings, I would not give *the* NIP *of a
ftraw* for our conftitution, in church and
ftate.

From the firft ages of Chriftianity, celibacy *(n)* in both fexes has been efteemed the
fublimity of virtue: its merit is derived

* See Review of the Cafe of the Diffenters, p. 22.

from

from the difficulty we feel, in this frail ſtate of mortality, in reſiſting the inſtinctive im-pulſe of animal ſenſation. Hence, the monaſtick life became early the divine teſt of corporeal purity, celeſtial fervour, and ſpiritual devotion. But theſe new reformers have raſhly abſolved both monks and nuns from the ſolemn vows by which they had devoted themſelves to heaven, and impiouſly encouraged them to abandon their peaceful and ſanctimonious retreats, and expoſe themſelves to the " pomps and " vanities of this wicked world, and the " ſinful luſts of the fleſh." However, it were well indeed if the miſchief ended here ;—but, alas ! this fatal ſtep will eventually prove the ruin of England, as it is calculated on the moſt moderate computation, that the fleets and armies of France may ſoon be manned and recruited from this new ſource of population. Their manufactures and agriculture will no longer be diſ-

treſſed

treffed by a war, as it may be carried on with vigour and facility without calling a fingle man from the plough or loom. Our moft experienced ftatefmen, our wifeft patriots, our moft enlightened fenators, are convinced of this melancholy truth : The French Revolution is therefore generally execrated; and has only received the contemptible plaudits of an obfcure fociety, compofed of atheiftical Diffenters, republican Deifts, and levelling Freethinkers, who impatiently long for the deftruction of our civil and ecclefiaftical eftablifhment.

The celebrated Mr. Necker has fagacioufly obferved, that it daily became more requifite than ever, to inculcate the genuine dictates of religion on the minds of the people, as the only effectual confolation to fupport them under the weight of oppreffive, unequal, and impoverifhing taxation (o). But the neceffity of enforcing this pious doctrine is unhappily done away,

as

as a redreſs of grievances and a reſtoration of rights have already taken place; and it is a melancholy truth, that reverſionary felicity makes but a ſlight impreſſion on thoſe who have a proſpect of enjoying the comforts of this life. The celeſtial ſpecifick ſo earneſtly recommended by Mr. Necker derives its vital efficacy from the exertions of arbitrary power, which compels us to purchaſe eternal joy by a few years miſery in this tranſitory ſtate of probation. The prieſthood, influenced by this ſacred motive, have ever been the zealous advocates of deſpotiſm, except when their own privileges and immunities are endangered; as in ſuch a predicament, they are precluded from exerciſing their own judgement, and only act as truſtees and delegates for the rights of heaven.

The late emperor, Joſeph the *Great*, who aſtoniſhed the world by the ſublimity of his genius and the grandeur of his actions,

2   not

not adverting to this political axiom,
feems to have committed a fatal error,
in not conciliating the affections, and fe-
curing the attachment of the church (and
perhaps the law) before he commenced
his comprehenfive and beneficent fyftem
of government in the Auftrian Nether-
lands.

Lord Stanhope has thought proper to pafs
an eulogy on the National Affembly, for
making no diftinction between Catholicks
and Proteftants, but impartially admitting
both to all offices of truft and profit; and invidioufly contrafts our conduct with their's
in refpect to the Diffenters. But if their
true motive be confidered, they will be
found by no means entitled to panegyrick.
By this affected moderation, this fpecious
candour, this comprehenfive indulgence,
they evidently exhibit a contemptuous indifference for the Catholick eftablifhed
church, and the folemn decifions of coun-
cils and theologifts. This is a dangerous
unequivocal

unequivocal fymptom of their malady—a prognoftick and a diagnoftick of Atheifm.

On the fame confiftency of principle, M. Mirabeau moved this fenate of *democrates* to addrefs the king to appoint an envoy for the fpecial purpofe of jointly confulting with our adminiftration on the moft effectual means of abolifhing the flave trade. Did this fpring from the generous fuggeftions of humanity? Certainly not.—Treachery marks their proceedings; and the ruin of revealed religion is the invariable aim of all their actions. For has it not been inconteftably proved, by writers* equally diftinguifhed by genius, learning, and profound refearches into antiquity, that the eldeft born of Ham, who was accurfed by his father, was called Cufh, " which, in the Hebrew language, fignifies black. Ethiopia, under which name Africa is included, is called in Scripture the Land of Cufh, and the inhabitants, Cufhims, or Cufhites.—The ne-

* Mr. Bryant, &c.

E   groes

groes therefore are defcended from Ham,
by his eldeft fon, Cufh; which accounts
for the degraded fituation thefe people have
ever continued in."—This reafoning is con-
clufive.—The Cufhites were certainly devoted to perpetual flavery, for the wickednefs of their great progenitor, Ham. Cufh
himfelf was probably born black, both as a
prophetick defignation of his future fate, and
to tranfmit this degenerate colour to his
pofterity.

The only fpecious objection to this very
rational hypothefis, is obviated by the author of *Obfervations*, &c. in anfwer to Mr.
Clarkfon's reprobated Effay. " It may be
objected," fays he, " that Cufh was born
prior to the time of Ham's committing the
offence againft his father, for which he fentenced him and his pofterity to fo fevere a
punifhment; and therefore the complexion
of Cufh could not have any relation to the
crime to be committed afterwards by his
father. In anfwer to this, I obferve, there

is

is no impropriety, nor improbability, in fuppofing that the blacknefs of Cufh was the mark fet upon him and his pofterity, from the foreknowledge of the Deity, of the crime, and confequent punifhment, which Ham would commit, and be fentenced to; and as a feal of that perpetual fervitude to which his defcendants were to be doomed by that fentence*." '

Be this as it may, it is inconteftibly proved by the celebrated author of *Ancient Mythology*, and univerfally admitted, that the Europeans are the fons of Japheth : it is therefore our indifpenfable duty to accomplifh the divine predictions of Noah, and to hold Ham's defcendants in chains for ever. But it is the avowed intention of the National Affembly to weaken the credibility of the facred hiftory, by emancipating the negroes. However, I truft we fhall not be made the dupes of this profane policy:

* Page 32

on

on the contrary, I fincerely wifh, that the corporations of Briftol and Liverpool would fend out the reverend author of the *Scriptural Refearches* * to the Weft-Indies, with a cargo of bibles; which may be conveniently ftowed in the flave-fhip, as they are not now fo much crowded as formerly. Let him teach the unfortunate Africans to read and ftudy the book of Genefis;—let *their* genealogy be condenfed into a fhort catechifm, fuited to their untutored capacities, and taught them every Sunday by one of the negro-divers.—It is impoffible to fay what a fudden and falutary effect it may have on their unenlightened minds, to *know* that their fufferings are folely owing to the wickednefs of their anceftor, Ham.

It will conciliate their affections, and endear the fons of Japheth to their hearts, if they are once perfuaded that we hold them in bondage, and inflict ftripes on them, neither to obtain any bafe and
fordid

* Rev. Mr. Herries.

fordid profit from their burning toils, nor to
gratify the fudden impulfe of vindictive paf-
fion, but merely in obedience to the decrees
of Heaven, to accomplifh the word of pro-
phecy, as faithful executors to the laft will
and teftament of Noah, our common proge-
nitors, the fecond father of mankind. *(p)*

Monf. Volney *, indeed, would fain per-
fuade us, on the authority of Herodotus,
that the Ægyptians, celebrated both in
profane and facred hiftory, were blacks;
and thence artfully infinuates, that we do
not abfolutely derive our intellectual fupe-
riority over them from the whitenefs of
our fkins. But, even on this hypothefis,
though the Ægyptians might have been of
a dark colour, yet they were not of fo deep
a die as the defcendants of Cufh, nor was

* Nam Colchi videntur Ægyptii effe.—Ipfe autem ex
hoc conjectabam, quod *atro colore* funt et *crifpo capillo,*
(μελανχροες και ѕλοτριχες.)

HEROD. l. 2, p. 211,—Glaf. ed.

their

their hair fo foft and woolly; which makes
an effential difference between them *(q)*. Befides, it has been conjectured by the Abbé
Spalanzani, and demonftrated by a late diffec-
tion at Jamaica, that the cellular membrane,
on which the colour of the epidermis or
outer cuticle depends, is wondroufly extended over the brain of the negroes, and
completely wraps up the *cerebrum* and *cere-
bellum* in its curious net-work. Confequently, the impreffion made by external
objects on the *fenforium* is rendered lefs dif-
tinct by paffing through this reticular *enve-
lope*, the nervous fenfibility thereby blunt-
ed, and the rational faculties weakened. By
this aftonifhing contexture of the reafoning
organ, the pofterity of Ham, and the fons
of Japheth, are fpecifically diftinguifhed
from each other; the former cannot feel
fo exquifitely as the latter, either intel-
lectually or fenfitively; and yet, by this
admirable contrivance, they are gracioufly
fitted

fitted for that ftate of degradation and flavery to which they are perpetually devoted.

It will give me great pleafure if this
fingular difcovery fhould afford the leaft
fatisfaction to thofe whofe generous but
mifapplied fympathy has carried them be-
yond all bounds of prudence and difcretion
on the fubject of the flave-trade. They
may now reft affured that the negroes
do not fuffer more than they can bear.—
The dullnefs of their underftandings, and
the bluntnefs of their fenfations, (origi-
nating from the fame caufe,) alleviate their
tranfient miferies, and proportionably fhield
and protect them from that pungency of men-
tal and corporeal pain they would otherwife
feel from incidental acts of feverity, to
which a ftate of flavery muft fometimes ex-
pofe them. This anatomical defcription of
the prolongation and extenfion of the fub-
cutaneous membrane over the brain, fhould
be explained to the blacks, in familiar un-
technical

technical language by the surgeon of the plantation, who charitably visits and attends them after every punishment; as they are always humanely indulged with some hours rest and relaxation, to repair their exhausted strength and spirits. When they have once attained a clear scientifick conception of this phenomenon from the surgeon, the clergyman should then explain the *final cause* of it to his catachumens, that they may derive religious consolation from this marked providential inferiority of their species, and look up to their masters, mistresses, and their kind guardians, the negro-drivers, with more awe and reverence.

The National Assembly, possessed by the same mischievous dæmon of democracy, have actually proceeded to abolish titles and reduce pensions.

I hope a few impartial reflections on this very interesting point, may in some measure obviate the pernicious tendency of such levelling republican notions.—As the French *nobleffe* always sacrificed to the graces, they

derived

derived their captivating politenefs, and in-
imitable addrefs, from the affiduity of this
pleafing devotion. They gave a decided
ton to fociety in exact proportion to the dif-
tinctions of rank and birth. A fimple
gentilhomme edged in, as he could, through
the half-opened door of a lady's affembly-
room; but whenever an archbifhop, a
prince of the blood, or an ambaffador,
was announced, " *ouvrez les deux battants
pour monfeign'. l'archeveque,*" &c. was the
fafhionable language. A nice and fafti-
dious obferver, who had been ufed to good
company, could inftantly difcover *duc et
pair,* a fimple duke, a marquis, a vifcount,
or count, by the condefcending hauteur,
the dignified familiarity, or graceful negli-
gence of returning a bow, or prefenting a
fnuff-box to an inferior, with as much
precifion as if he had examined their
refpective patents. But all thefe enchanting accomplifhments will be foon
neglected. The eye of tafte will fpeedily
lofe this exquifite difcrimination, which

F   was

was never before attained in ancient or modern times. *L'amour, la chaffe, le fervice, l'agrément de la focieté, les mots heureux, les petits foins,* will give place to the *trifteffe* of party and the *ennui* of politicks, to the tumults of faction and the conflicts of ambition. The gay and feducing attendance of the toilet will be deferted for the fenate ; and a tedious debate on the conftitution will arreft the attention more than a new dance at the opera, or a ballet at Verfailles. A poetical *ariftocrate* who feels for the *decadence* of his country, laments this fatal change of manners in the following pathetick and affecting lines :

" Autrefois, dans la France,
" La prefence d'un duc faifoit taire un marquis :
" Devant l'homme à la cour admis
" Un gentilhomme de province
" N'auroit ofè refter affis.
" Un bourgeois refpectoit le noble le plus mince ;
" Les plus grands impofoient toujours aux plus petits ;
" Et c'etoit un ordre admirable :
" Mais l' aujourdhui dans ce Paris
" C' eft un defpotifme effroyable ; .
" *Tout le monde y dit fon avis* *."

* *Reveil d'Epeminide.*

How

How different is our fituation at this moment! how triumphant the contraft! By
the aufpicious exercife of the prerogative,
the Britifh and Irifh peerage have been
liberally increafed during the prefent
reign.—As birth, fortune, and defert are
not faftidioufly deemed indifpenfible qualifications, the gratitude of the new peer to
the crown is infured, as he can only afcribe
his promotion to the gracious favour of his
fovereign, and the benign influence of the
minifter. Thus the pride and arrogance of
affuming merit are effectually checked; and
a courtly complaifant race of nobles gradu-
ally formed; all actuated by the true fpirit
of ariftocracy, and implicitly devoted to
the crown; always ready to fupport its
prerogatives, and maintain the fplendid privileges of their own order, againft vulgar
prejudice, and popular encroachments.

For though the lords derive their honour
from the crown, the fountain of all honour;

ftill

ftill as they are only truftees, they fhould be ever ready to refign it with alacrity on any great political crifis. By a fpirited exertion, founded on this generous fentiment, a few noble peers, (if report is to be credited) gallantly defpifing reproach and obloquy, and difdaining to be bound by too rigid and fcrupulous an adherence to their word, faved the king, the church, and the nation, by voting againft the Eaft India bill in 1783.

On the fame maxim, a defertion of friends, party, and principle, may fometimes be confidered as a political teft, and as a juft, fair, and conftitutional claim to a penfion and peerage; being a fort of feudal homage, and the moft unequivocal proof of profound duty, loyalty, and attachment. Surely even the malignity of faction muft admit, that the elevation of foul which indignant virtue infpires, could alone induce any perfon to act what is commonly, but very erroneoufly, deemed a difhonourable part

in

in politicks.—Would the moſt unprinci-
pled adminiſtration abandon ſuch an in-
trepid convert, to be vilified, traduced, and
expoſed to the bitter taunts, and contemptuous ſneers of a calumniating oppoſition?
No: let a man of ſuch heroick merit never be
conſigned to diſgrace; let him be enobled by
a title, and enriched by a penſion, in order
to excite a generous emulation in others,
and as the only adequate reward and conſolation he himſelf can reliſh.

I have alſo, Sir, often reflected with ſin-
gular ſatisfaction on the pleaſing mode in
which civil ſuits were carried on in France;
where even the deciſions of juſtice were
biaſſed by the gentle influence of manners and cuſtoms, and blended with their
ſocial ſyſtem of policy. The *Preſident* was
uſually ſolicited in perſon, by his noble or
fair clients; and their ſtate of the caſe was
liſtened to with the moſt polite reſpect and
attention. As gallantry and law were happily

pily united, ladies with great condefcenfion
vifited the judge at his own chamber.—
When beauty pleaded her caufe irrefifti-
bly in private, what a faint impreffion
could even the eloquence of an Erfkine
make in open court? Sometimes an amorous propofition, expreffed with the utmoft
delicacy, dropped from the judge, and if
favourably received, *le proces etoit gagné*. A
French critick has produced a fpecimen of
elegant wit, addreffed by a judicial magiftrate to a charming fuitor, on this nice
point, equally honourable to himfelf and
the jurifprudence of his country : The *equi-
voque* of a legal term is happily preferved ;
for as the author was a lawyer, he remem-
bered the profeffion in his poetical rapture,
and refted his claim to *reciprocity* on a *double
entendre :*

" Vous avez chez moi libre *acces*,
" J'en demande chez vous un *autre*. .
" Si je ne gagne mon proces,
" Vous ne gagnerez pas ie votre:" &c.

But

But the barbarous fpirit of democracy has interrupted this tender intercourfe! this fentimental mode of conducting law-fuits! The fale of judicial offices will no longer be permitted. A previous ftudy and long practice in the courts will be efteemed indifpenfible qualifications for the bench; and confequently young men will be excluded, on whofe generous feelings the tears and follicitations of the fair never fail to excite the warmeft emotions.—Inexorable *bourgeois* juries will be eftablifhed, who may prefume to judge both of the law and fact; no deference will be paid to birth, rank, or riches; and an accomplifhed courtier, perhaps a favourite of his fovereign, will be treated like one of the *canaille.* But the evil will not ftop here: not only the foft intercourfe which has been juft defcribed, will no longer be tolerated, but all the delicacies of *politeffe* will be abolifhed, and ancient rufticity revived.

" The

" The ideas which the Greeks formed
of politenefs, muft have been very different from ours," fays Mr. Hume, in
quoting this paffage from Menander: " It
is not in the power of the Gods to make
a polite foldier." The reafon is obvious.—
The turbulent fpirit of licentious equality
diffufed among the Grecian republicks, in-
fpired a contempt for thofe finer focial arts,
the original invention of which even Mr.
Dutens admits to be modern. They difdained to acquire that refpectful addrefs, that de-
licate adulation, and honourable fubferviency
to the pleafure and inclination of others, in
which the very effence of true politenefs confifts. Such a fenfitive plant fhrinks from
the rough hand of democracy, and can be
only cultivated to its utmoft perfection
under the genial influence and cheering
beams of court funfhine. The author of
Efprit des Loix, who faw this finely ex
emplified in his own country, remarks,
with

with patriotick exultation, "that politeneſs and arbitrary power made an equal pro-greſs among the Romans." The converſe of this propoſition is likewiſe true. The French will ſoon loſe that boaſted ſupe-riority which has ſo long excited the envy and emulation of Europe. Even the Dutch, under the auſpicious protection of the Pruſſian monarch, will ſpeedily be *drilled* into more refinement, and excel them in every graceful and elegant accompliſhment. As amiableneſs of character is attained by the agreeable art of concealing the boiſterous ſallies of paſſion, and reſtraining the diſ-guſting bluntneſs of ſincerity, politeneſs and diſſimulation are indiſſolubly con-nected, and always flouriſh under the pro-tection of royalty. This exterior varniſh pleaſes the eye, though it diſguiſes the heart;—as painting glaſs, beautifies it, but renders it leſs tranſparent.

Thus the ſplendour of ariſtocracy was

G   diffuſed

diffufed to the wideft extent in France, was protracted through every gradation of fo-ciety, and threw a brilliancy over their do-meftick manners. The fovereign difpofed of the whole national revenue, and difpofed of it with the moft judicious liberality.—Thofe who were incapable of affifting themfelves,—thofe who could no longer afford the indulgence of fafhionable ex-pence,—thofe who difdained to tarnifh the luftre of their birth by the fordid acqui-fition of commercial gain,—ftill enjoyed every luxury of life, by the condefcending kindnefs of royal beneficence. A million and a half (almoft the twelfth of the whole product of national taxation) was gracioufly beftowed, with unbounded generofity, on a fuperb and gallant race of nobles. As this mine of regal munificence was ex-hauftlefs, Paris and Verfailles were crowded by men of fhining accomplifhments, who, with paffionate anxiety, longed to recommend

mend themſelves at court. But it was neither by the arrogance of ſelf-aſſumed merit,
nor the revolting pride of parts, that their
hopes were to be realized, and their wiſhes
gratified. Where the faſcinating influence,
diſcriminating taſte, and deciſive power of
the fair ſex prevailed, their favourites roſe
to fame and fortune, by the acquiſition of
thoſe artificial embelliſhments, and by
that exquiſite poliſh, which the *taƐt fin*
of Verſailles could alone appretiate. No
envoy was appointed to a foreign court
who could not trace the complicated figure
of a minuet with graceful preciſion. The
dignified credentials of an ambaſſador were
often granted for the compoſition of a
chanſon amoureuſe; and *de pincer la harpe
avec gout,* or to poſſeſs the happy art *de
bien tourner ſon compliment,* has frequently raiſed an officer to the command of
an army, or a clerk in office to preſide
over the marine of France. War or peace

depended

depended on the charming caprice, on the
fmile or frown of this enchanting gyno-
cracy; and the *beaux yeux* of the reigning
Sultana often fet the world in a blaze.

The faucy indifcretion of ill-bred authors
was likewife inftantly correfted, and an
inftrudtive hint conveyed to them in the
polite ftyle of a *lettre de cachet.*—Diderot
was treated with this flattering mark of attention by Madame de Pompadour, and fent
to apartments provided for him by the king
at *Vincennes,* for prefuming to criticife the
compofition and execution of a favourite
court fiddler, without being himfelf a con-
noiffeur in mufick. Rouffeau, with his accuftomed mifanthropy, prefented a *memoire,*
foliciting the enlargement of his friend, or
requefting to fhare his prifon*. Both thefe
favours were, with great propriety, refufed
him; yet he ungratefully exercifed his cy-
nical declamation, on not being indulged in
either alternative,

Lettres

* Confeffions de Rouffeau, tom 2,

Lettres de cachet were also frequently issued, out of pure tenderness to husbands, who, left they should be eye-witnesses to the intrigues of their wives, were kindly rescued from domestick distress, and shut up in the *Bastile,* where they enjoyed every comfort of life, without anxiety or trouble. This indulgence was usually granted at the solicitation of the lover, who evinced his passion to his mistress, and his friendship to her spouse, by the same act. A handsome *bourgeoise* was always sure of attracting the gallant attention of some young and amorous courtier; and the confinement of her husband was the natural consequence : but now he will have the mortification of constantly beholding the indiscretion of his wife; as his house will be deemed his castle, from which he cannot be removed without a formal process of law.

But, alas! the whole of this sublime and beautiful system is deranged. The very

dregs

dregs of the people have fatally difcovered that nobles, princes, and even kings, are formed of the fame clay with themfelves, and owe their elevation and grandeur only to the accidental circumftances of birth and fortune. It has been well obferved, that truth fhould not be told at all times; and fure a truth of this dangerous tendency fhould ever be concealed from the vulgar; for contempt often begins with them when admiration ceafes. They were happy and content when they looked up to the great ones of the earth, as beings of a fuperior order; but the pleafing delufion from whence they enjoyed fo much felicity will quickly vanifh; the tranfient fplendour of a terreftial meteor would no longer excite their wonder and aftonifhment, if they did not trace its origin to the heavens, and miftake it for a falling ftar.

I am confirmed in the juftice of thefe fentiments by the philofophical obfervations of

Mr.

Mr. Necker, who defcribes, with fympathe-
tick delight, the happinefs of the French peafantry before the late political revolution.
" They behold," fays he, " the oftentatious
difplay of ranks with the cooleft indifference; grandeur is fo remote from their ha-
bitual ideas, that they accuftom themfelves
to look upon it as the attribute of a few beings of a fpecies different from their's ; and
as they return home to their cottages, under
the preffure of a burthen they can fcarcely
bear, they fee thofe fiery courfers, who ra-
pidly whirl the magnificent chariots of the
rich and noble, clofe by them, and view
them with the fame indifference as they
contemplate thofe wandering planets over
their heads, whofe twinkling motion they
juft difcern." But this beautiful Arcadian
landfcape will quickly vanifh ; the ferenity
of their prefent enjoyments will fpeedily
be difturbed ; their political confequence in
elections will excite new and afpiring ideas,

and

and foon transform this humble, contented, fubmiffive peafantry, into a bold, turbulent, factious yeomanry; thofe magnificent
chariots and fiery courfers will ftop at their
doors, and the rich and great will conde-
fcendingly alight to follicit their votes; they
will be tempted, by long leafes and low
rents, to lead a life of care, anxiety, and
labour, in the cultivation of the farms.
The *taille (r)*, that excellent tax, fo admira-
bly calculated to maintain the fplendour and
dignity of the *nobleffe*, and keep their te-
nantry in a comfortable ftate of degradation,
will be abolifhed for ever. They will fpurn
their vegetable meal, and infolently, perhaps, afpire to realize the unkingly wifh of
Henri quatre, whofe ftatue is ftill contemptuoufly exhibited on the *Pont Neuf*, as a mo-
nument of his folly;—" That he hoped to
fee the time when every peafant in France
fhould eat flefh meat once a day, and have a
boiled fowl for his Sunday's dinner."

The

The more I consider this important subject, the political evils that menace our
country, from the fatal revolution in
France, become more apparent. I shall
adduce one striking instance by which our
revenue and manufactures may be ruined.
The *commutation act* is now a favourite
one, as it fairly and impartially compels
every man to pay an additional window tax,
in order to reduce the price of tea: if he
does not choose to drink it, he has no reafon to complain, as it is his own fault.
Perhaps it will be suggested at some moment of popular frenzy, that the commutation act is a badge of slavery; for
when this measure was first proposed, it
was compared in debate to the *gabelle*, a similar fort of impost on salt, which long
prevailed in France, and has lately been
abolished by the National Affembly. Mr.
Fox, though he owned the justness of the
remark, factiously preferred the mild spirit

H   of

of French taxation; afferting, " that there was no degree of comparifon, on the plea of neceffity; between the ufe of falt and tea.—The latter was clearly a luxury, and no ways conducive to health; perhaps far otherwife, as many had thought. Salt, on the contrary, was a neceffary; and therefore it was far lefs oppreffive to oblige the fubjects of France to purchafe as much falt as it was fuppofed a perfon of any given defcription in life would have occafion for." Thefe words may be malicioufly repeated, to excite fedition and difloyalty in the minds of the people, and induce them to infift on the repeal of a moft equitable and impartial tax.—What muft be the confequence? The flourifhing ftate of the Eaft-India Company would no longer excite Mr. Crawford's admiration; bankruptcy muft enfue; publick credit would be fhaken; the rapid reduction of the national debt

would

would ceafe; and we fhould no longer be charmed by the accuracy of calculation and elegance of compofition, fo eminently difplayed in that annual oration, (the India budget) which fhews forth the merit, and celebrates the praife, of the prefident and members of the board of control.

The dangerous proximity of the two countries alfo makes me tremble.—Our manufacturers, on any wife judicious extenfion of the excife laws, will be tempted to migrate to France, inftead of doubling their induftry and fharpening their ingenuity here, both to pay the tax and evade the law. Now, as our experienced and enlightened minifters have candidly declared, that all our future refources of revenue, all our hopes of a permanent flourifhing finance, muft be derived from an extenfion of our excife laws, and their application to our manufactures, we may be reduced to the melancholy alternative of choofing either to

be

be ruined by enforcing, or abandoning, this salutary syftem. The threats and audacious conduct of the tobacconifts at this moment, implicitly directed by the factious advice of an able, active, and dangerous leader in the houfe of commons, furnifh too lamentable a proof of the facility with which our fraudulent fmuggling traders (moft of whom are diffenters) may be induced to fpurn at the laws of their country, elude the wifdom of its acts; and, with unparalleled impudence, to combat and oppofe the opinion both of the minifter and his fecretary.

The moft effectual means fhould be inftantly purfued to check this growing mifchief; and perhaps none could be better than re-eftablifhing the obfolete practice of iffuing *general warrants,* at the difcretion of the fecretary of ftate. If there fhould ftill remain any abfurd prejudice againft the name, let them be called *lettres de cachet.*

A late

A late eminent magiftrate * recommended the adoption of this meafure, with great force of reafoning, and unanfwerable argument, in order to check the migration of our manufacturers, and the export of our *fpinning-Jennys:* but now the French revolution, and the wife extenfion of our excife laws, have made it not only prudent, but abfolutely neceffary for the prefervation of the empire. The prefent member for Middlefex has a glorious opportunity of making the *amende honorable* to his king, country, and conftituents, by bringing in a bill to *legalize* general warrants, or *lettres de cachet.* Let the commons pafs it, and the lords will not venture to throw it out. The daring menaces of the tobacconifts, in their evidence, may ferve as a preamble to the act; and a fpecial claufe may be inferted to fufpend the pernicious operation of the *habeas corpus* act for feven

---

* Sir John Hawkins. Life of Dr. Johnfon, p. 510.

years;

years; and at the end of that time it will be totally forgot.

In ſhort, the expediency of ſtrengthening the arm of executive power is univerſally admitted; and as we have hitherto derived all our riches, glory, and happineſs, by keeping up a cordial enmity, and provoking rivalſhip between us and France, by a total diverſity of laws, opinions, and conſtitution; let us ſtill, with patriotick pertinacity, adhere to our old ſyſtem, and we may yet bid defiance to all our enemies, foreign and domeſtick. On this principle, the following hints may be of uſe.—

Let the whole of the Britiſh revenue be farmed to that great *controller* of finance, Monſ. C. Let a royal *imprimatur* be eſtabliſhed; (nibbling at the newſpapers, by forbidding them to be *lent*, is a nugatory policy;) let both houſes of convocation meet to recommend lotteries, and his majeſty's proclamation for the reformation of manners;

ners; let them appoint a committee, (Doctor H. in the chair) to cite, degrade, and deprive such of the clergy of their benefices who shall presume to support any of the present members of the house of commons, at the next general election, who voted for a repeal of the test act; let them examine, and sentence to the flames, all publications of an immoral tendency, and commit the authors, printers, and readers to Newgate; let the schism bill, which expired on the 1st of August 1714, be revived; let the authority of the bishops' court be extended, and no appeal allowed from their decisions, except to heaven. Something of this sort has been already done, just sufficient to provoke the animadversions of Doctor Price; and what more can be said in praise of administration?

Even you, Sir, must acknowledge that I spread no false alarm, when we are at this moment menaced with a restoration of the

pagan

pagan divinities. The Pantheon may receive the gods of Greece and Rome; and perhaps we may fee the worſhip which has been very lately aboliſhed at Iſernia, revived at Ranelagh. Our youth are early initiated into the myſteries of the heathen mythology, and have too ſtrong a propenſity to kneel at the ſhrine of Venus, and pour out libations to Bacchus. In ſhort, the revolution in France, the ſpirit of the diſſenters, and the licentious wiſh of a platonick philoſopher *(s)*, ſtrike me with the utmoſt horror. The approaching calamities of Britain lie heavy on my heart. At all events, I ſhall endeavour to act with fortitude and reſignation :

" Such in thoſe moments, as in all the paſt,
" O fave my country, Heaven, ſhall be my laſt."

But a conſideration of the utmoſt importance yet remains. The dangerous revolt of the military, on whom the ſtability and glory of theFrench monarchy reſted, has excited my
indignation,

indignation, and almost driven me to despair. If soldiers once presume to consider themselves as citizens, to enter into any discussion and distinctions on this invidious subject, there will be no use in keeping up those large standing armies, to which modern governments owe their brilliancy and power.—No similar instance has happened since the year 1688.—" James drew out his army," says Lord Bolingbroke, " but in vain, for it was an English one." Louis did not draw out his army, for it was no longer a French one! And thus kings have been deserted, and delivered up into the hands of their revolted subjects, and a fatal revolution brought about in France and England, by the shameful defection of the troops. But an extension of the evil is still to be dreaded, and has already taken effect. Papers, called *le Soldat Patriotique*, are dispersed among the military on the continent, exciting the privates of every battallion to

I   mutiny

mutiny; and tauntingly afking them, whether they are not degraded, by fubmitting
to the caprice of puerile *ariflocrates*, who are
wifely commiffioned by their fovereign to
drill and chaftife them into military difcipline, by the magical effects of a *ratan?*
Thefe inflammatory addreffes have already
had fuch a fatal operation, that I queftion
whether a German prince could now induce
his troops, by double pay, to fulfil a con-
tract with *us* or Spain, if the flame of rebellion fhould fpread to her colonies in South
America, or to the Ifle of Man.

On the whole, Sir, I own myfelf terrified
at the very idea of innovation. The fer-
mentation of democracy, begun in France,
may extend here, and excite a fatal change
in our tempers and difpofitions. Your
philofophical purfuits incline you to be
lefs tremblingly apprehenfive; you falfe-
ly conclude from analogy, that our conftitution may be improved by imprégnating

it

it with a new principle, as you have given common water the fpirit and flavour of Pyrmont, by a lucky infufion of fixed air-But the ancients were wifely, and even timidly circumfpect on this effential point of policy. The kings and ephori of Sparta have juftly merited and obtained the praifes of all pofterity for iffuing a decree againft Timotheus, and fining him, for adding another ftring to the harp. Thofe profound judges of human nature inftantly perceived that the laws and inftitutions of Lycurgus would foon be rendered inefficacious by the wanton vibrations excited in the ears of their fober and uncorrupted youth, by this unconftitutional ftring. They exprefsly fay, " He has given to our mufick an effeminate and artificial drefs, inftead of the plain and orderly one in which it has hitherto appeared ; rendering melody infamous, by compofing in the *chromatick*, inftead of the *enharmonick*. Be it therefore

enacted,

enacted, by the authority aforefaid, that Timotheus be banifhed from our city, that men may be warned for the future not to introduce any *innovation* * into Sparta!"

I only quote this very fingular hiftorical anecdote, to convince our felf-opiniated, fceptical reformers, that nothing was deemed trifling by the wifdom of antiquity which could in the flighteft degree tend to any alteration in the government.

In the prefent wildnefs of political fpeculation in France, I fhould not be furprifed if fome declaiming demagogue propofed the eating of raw flefh, *a la mode d'Abyffinie,* in order to keep up the rage and violence of the commons in unabated vigour. An act of the National Affembly (confidering their unhappy influence) would foon make this favage cuftom fafhionable, under the fallacious pretence of reducing the price of

---

* Burney's Hiftory of Mufic, vol. 1, p. 408.

wood;

wood; and rendering one article of the commercial treaty of no effect, by preventing the importation of coals. This barbarous nutriment would soon be relished here, as we have always had a propensity to that sort of food; and would infallibly produce every atrocious act of ferocity which has already desolated that devoted land.

As the passions, taste, and appetites, principally originate from the physical properties of our diet, our virtues and vices may be traced to the same source, and improved, or counteracted, by a moral regimen. This sentiment is neither new nor paradoxical; it has been already elucidated, with philosophick truth and poetical beauty, by one of our most elegant and pleasing poets:

" Was ever Tartar fierce or cruel
" Upon the strength of water gruel?
" But who shall stand his rage and force,
" If first he rides, then eats his horse *."

* Prior's *Alma.*

The

The cruelty or mildnefs of animals depends on their either being graminivorous or carnivorous; man, by his dignified nature, enjoys the optional privilege of being either; but as he is alfo diftinguifhed by the fuperior faculty of *cooking* *, the direful effects of a raw-flefh diet are counteracted by this humane refinement. The Hindoos are meek, gentle, uncommonly patient, and fubmit to every act of extortion and rapine, with aftonifhing compofure and the moft laudable refignation. Our countrymen, who, by their travels and indefatigable refearches, have acquired a perfect and accurate knowledge of Indoftan, all agree (however they may differ on other points) in giving the natives this very amiable character, and univerfally afcribe it to their fimple vegetable diet. This phyfical principle is fo well underftood, that the

---

* See Bofwell's *Tour to the Hebrides*, 3d edit. p. 21, note.

2   fighting

fighting *cafts* are compelled to eat flefh, as an effential part of military difcipline; otherwife they would foon lofe their courage and the *efprit de corps*, and meanly degenerate into the tamenefs of mere citizens.

I could adduce ftrong reafons for throwing out this alarming hint, and have now in my poffeffion letters from a leading member of the National Affembly, to prove that this horrid fcheme is in agitation. The vanity of Frenchmen induces them to think, that as they have long given the *ton, enfait de manger*, the moft ariftocratick people in Europe (even Spaniards and Germans) will foon eat themfelves into a republican frenzy, as they will be ftimulated by a frefh incenfive at every meal. This is the favourite project of our reftlefs and ambitious rivals at prefent, who ftill vainly flatter themfelves with the hope of eftablifhing a fhocking fyftem of univerfal democracy, by this infamous expedient

Our

Our beſt preſervative, in ſuch an emer-
gency, would be a general teſt act, depriving every man of the rights and privileges of a citizen, beſides ſubjecting him
to a fine, at the diſcretion of the judges,
and impriſonment till it was paid, who
did not produce and lodge a certificate
weekly at the exciſe office, ſigned by the
rector, curate, and church-wardens of the
pariſh, certifying his exact compliance with
the obligatory clauſes of the ſaid act, *to
wit*, " That A. or B. had duly and regu-
larly eaten his fleſh or fiſh, either boiled,
roaſted, baked, broiled, or fryed." Yet I
am fully perſuaded, that you, Sir, and your
brethren, the diſſenters, would ſtill remain
ſtubborn and refractory, and factiouſly complain of this ſalutary reſtraint, as a new
grievance, and again expatiate on the natural and abſtract rights of man, to eat his
meat according to his own whim, either
raw or roaſted.

If

If experiments in every branch of medical philofophy were purfued on a liberal and comprehenfive plan, new fources of knowledge would be opened for our contemplation, and the evils of life greatly alleviated. The late Doctor Johnfon's fpeculations on this fubject were new and curious. I remember when the fcheme of fending Swifs troops to the Eaft Indies was talked of, a perfon in converfation cenfured it, becaufe on foreign fervice they are liable to the *maladie du pays*, and often languifh away their lives, unlefs they are permitted to return home. The Doctor afked, whether there were any Scotch regiments in India? On being anfwerd in the affirmative,—" Let the Switzers, then," faid he, " be *inoculated* with the Scotch, and, rely on't, the difeafe will never reach them."

But, Sir, notwithftanding the ftrong fymptoms of our approaching ruin, I rejoice

K   joice

joice to fee a revival of our ancient fpirit.
The corporation and teft acts have not been
repealed; *elfe* infurrection, irreligion, and
anarchy, would have been the confequence.
Thofe acts are our defence againft the
encroachments of non-conformity;—they
are the fhield of our faith, which protects
us, againft the darts of fanaticifm. What
is the prefbyterian plea of merit? The
ftorm that overturned the church and ftate
was raifed by you; otherwife we fhould
have enjoyed at this moment the bleffed
calm of arbitrary power; for it was a
meritorious device in the clergy to convert, by a fpecies of political tranfubftan-
tiation, that implicit obedience they owed
the pope, into an unlimited allegiance
to the king: " And thus," fays the
farcaftick Doctor Hurd *, " arofe in the
church that pernicious fyftem of divine in-
defeafable right, broached indeed by the

* Moral and Political Dialogues.

clergy,

clergy, but not from thofe corrupt and temporary views to which it has been imputed." Sir John Maynard betrays the virulence of a whig, in his anfwer.—" This apology," fays he, " is the beft that could be made for them; but when one confiders the baneful tendency of thofe doctrines which were calculated to enflave the fouls and confciences of men, and, by advancing princes into the rank of gods, to juftify their tyranny, one cannot help feeling a ftrong refentment againft the teachers of them, however they themfelves might be impofed on by feveral colourable pretences."

It is my boaft, Sir, to have already demonftrated the effential benefits refulting from defpotifm and perfecution, and to have fhewn the hierarchy in a true light, confiftently labouring to promote both: I therefore truft thofe unfounded afperfions which have unguardedly dropt from the pen of the Bifhop of Worcefter, will have

K 2   little

little weight with the candid reader. Let
us now advert to the conduct of the diffenters at that critical period.—It is thus
defcribed by Mr. Hume, with whiggifh
rancour, and fanatical partiality:—" Any
word or writing which tended towards he-
refy, fchifm, or fedition," fays he, " was
punifhed by the high commiffioners, or any
three of them. They alone were judges of
whatever expreffions had that tendency;—
they proceeded not by information, but
upon rumour, fufpicion, or according to
their own fancy! The *puritanical* party,
though difguifed, [men of *clofe* ambition,]
had a very great authority over the kingdom ; and many of the leaders among the
commons had embraced the tenets of that
fect. All thefe were difgufted with the court,
both by the prevalence of civil liberty *effential to their party*, and on account of the re-
ftraints under which they were held by the
eftablifhed hierarchy." Thus the virtuous
austerity

aufterity of Archbifhop Laud, and the un-
fhaken attachment of Charles to epifcopacy,
were fatally counteracted by the rebellious
difpofition of the diffenters; otherwife we
fhould have had an holy inquifitorial tri-
bunal to watch over our morals, and re-
gulate our confciences, at this day.

Is it furprifing, then, that you are held
in abhorrence by the dignitaries of the
church? They have been roufed from their
lethargy; they no longer flumber in their
ftalls; they have been convened "from the
four quarters of the heavens" to ftigmatife
your proceedings. Like the Jewifh priefts *
of old, who enjoyed the exclufive privilege
of blowing the facred trumpet, Doctor H.
has founded an alarm from Mount *Sion*,
and gathered the elect together, to avenge
themfelves of their enemies.

"—— Quo non præftantius alter
" Ære ciere viros, martenique accendere cantu."

VIRGIL,

* Numbers, x. 8.

Have

Have you not, Sir, avowed the fame principles with your anceftors? and do you not
well deferve a fimilar treatment? I fee the
genuine fpirit of the primitive church revive, and the prefent race of diffenters are
the object of its wrath. Such pious fer-
vency was never equalled, except by the
orthodox zeal of the planters at Jamaica,
who, about a century ago, petitioned King
William " to banifh the Jews from that
ifland, becaufe they were the defcendants
of the crucifiers of our lord *."

" Ill will to the eftablifhment, muft
in all governments belong to a diffenter,
if he be an honeft man," fays a reverend
prelate †; " the man himfelf all the while
believes he is doing God and his country
fervice, and the harm that he may do under

* Hiftory of Jamaica, vol. 2, p. 293,
† Review of the Cafe of the Proteftant Diffenters, p. 14.
See alfo Bifhop Bonner's Comment on the Statute *de
Comburendis Hereticis*; where the fame fentiment is ably
maintained, and finely illuftrated.

this

this notion, will be only fo much the more, the greater we fuppofe his virtue and abilities." This impreffive truth cannot but have great weight with the publick, when the moral character of the diffenters is confidered; if they were vicious and profligate, there would be lefs danger.

It was confidently, indeed, afferted in debate, by Mr. Fox, that " it was neither juft nor candid to charge the diffenters with defigns which both their conduct and profeffions contradict. On this fallacious ground," fays he, " every fpecies of perfecution, from the maffacre of St. Bartholomew down to the corporation and teft act, may be juftified." Such arguments are clearly erroneous; yet they are always fet off by this fubdolous orator with fuch delufive ability, energy of expreffion, and impofing candour, that they too often make a fatal impreffion on the houfe. Hence his powers of deception; his pofitions being

2   frequently

frequently admitted as true, even on points of law and the practice of the courts, though contrary to the opinion of the most eminent lawyers, who generally neglect or disdain to answer him. Yet, in defiance of this specious logick, I still say, that the protestant dissenters have entered into a solemn league and covenant to destroy our civil and ecclesiastical establishment because I would do so in a similar situation; therefore I hate and persecute them, perfectly convinced I should merit the same treatment myself. Is not this strictly fulfilling that divine precept, of doing to all men what I would they should do unto me? This internal conviction, (as Hobbes finely observes,) from the very constitution of human nature, must operate stronger on me than either the conduct or professions of the dissenters. Allow me to elucidate this by a familiar instance:—Let us suppose a criminal arraigned at the Old-Bailey; may not the jury conscientiously

conclude,

conclude, that if they had been in the *same* situation with the prisoner, they would have committed the *same* crime; and therefore find him guilty, though contrary both to fact and evidence, and notwithstanding the culprit's solemn asseveration of his innocence.

On this principle I join issue with Mr. Fox, and assert with him, that the same orthodox argument justifies every species of persecution; therefore I have made it the foundation of all my reasoning on this misrepresented and mistaken subject.

The example of Ireland has been alledged, as a triumphant instance of no bad consequences having ensued from a repeal of the test act: but to this a most satisfactory answer has been given by the author of *A Review of the Case of the Dissenters.*—" The repeal of the Irish test act, in 1779, was probably," says he, " occasioned by the dread of a Spanish invasion. But what is the true use of Ireland's example?

L

ple? Eleven years are not yet paffed over fince the repeal took place. Is the repeal of the teft act juftified as a political meafure, or is it not, by the prefent fituation of the church and kingdom? Let the queftion fleep; its difcuffion might be more unpleafant than it could be profitable. *But let Great Britan beware.*"

I am extremely glad that Doctor H. has boldly and openly alluded to the treafonable negociation carried on between Spain and the diffenters of Ulfter, in 1779, as the Irifh fectaries are very irritable, and fore on this tender point. The fact is, that a fynod, denominated the *Northern Affociation,* was affembled at Belfaft, and fome propofitions actually moved, for delivering up the province and the linen manufacture to Spain, if government any longer oppofed the repeal of the teft act. It is reported, that Mr. Fletcher (who recently faved the church and ftate, by difclofing the dreadful

5

confpiracy

conspiracy of the diffenting ministers at Bol-
ton, in Lancashire,) was providentially a
member of the Irish synod; and secretly
withdrawing himself from the assembly, he
took post, arrived in a few hours at Dublin
castle, and laid this alarming intelligence
before the Lord Lieutenant.—A council was
suddenly called, and the heads of a bill drawn
up and certified, (Poyning's excellent law
being then in force,) and transmitted to
England, for a repeal of the test act.—A
copy was dispatched to the synod, entreat-
ing them at the same time to break off all
negociation with Spain. After some debate,
their request was complied with, and the
motions of the combined fleets in the chan-
nel became very languid, as Count d'Orvil-
liers' projects were utterly disconcerted by
this wise and judicious measure. The original papers, and the whole of the corre-
spondence between the president of the synod
and the Marquis del C——, I hear, will be

published

publifhed by the Bifhop of St. David's, as an appendix to his next edition of " A Review of the Cafe*."

Now, fir, permit me to afk you a plain queftion:—Does not the church fet an example to the diffenters how they fhould conduct themfelves on cafuiftical difficulties? Is it not perfectly underftood, that numbers of the clergy ardently wifh to be relieved from fubfcription to the thirty-nine articles, and fome years ago ftated their reafons, with great force and precifion, in a petition to the houfe of commons? Yet, as the legiflature did not think proper to comply with their requeft, they fubmit patiently, and confider the coercion of the fubfifting law as an ample juftification for their involuntary acquiefcence.

* This reverend prelate's zeal is a ftriking exemplification of a beautiful paffage in Doctor P——'s fermon, preached at the funeral of Archbifhop Secker, where he fays, " that could the world but fee the haraffing cares, which torment their bofoms, their perpetual anxieties, and diftreffing apprehenfions for the fouls of thofe committed to their care, BISHOPS need not be envied their coaches, their emoluments, their titles, or their dignitaries."

They

They conceive obedience, and holding their livings, to be their primary indifpenfible duty, even on the tenure of fubfcription to articles which they do not believe.—Yet they ftill maintain their confcientious objections in theory, and exhibit a laudable ingenuity, by reconciling unfullied principle with worldly wifdom: this is indeed fulfilling the fcripture, *be ye wife as ferpents and innocent as doves.*

Oaths are taken, and their obligation examined by them, with the fame candour and liberality, on the incontrovertible maxims of moral and political philofophy, fo ably illuftrated by Archdeacon Paley, who fhrewdly obferves, " That members of colleges, and other ancient foundations, are ftill required to fwear to the obfervance of their refpective ftatutes; which obfervance is become in fome cafes *unlawful,* in others *impracticable,* in others *ufelefs,* in others *inconvenient* *." But, if the act you fwear

* *Principles of Moral and Political Philofophy,* Vol. I. c. 21, p. 215. 5th edit.

to perform be abfurd and impracticable, you are, *ipfo facto,* abfolved at the moment you take it. So, if the caufe for prefcribing the oath originally no longer exifts, you are equally abfolved, as the effect necefFarily ceafes with the caufe. If the fpecifick acts enjoined are impracticable or abfurd, you virtually and truly comply with the genuine fpirit of the oath, as far as you poffibly can;—which is the utmoft you could do, even if you ftrictly and literally fulfilled every injunction, fuppofing they were neither abfurd or impracticable. It may be invidioufly afked, then, where is the utility of fuch a folemn appeal to Heaven ? and whether it would not be better either to form practicable oaths, or difpenfe with impracticable ones ? My conftant anfwer is—the danger to be apprehended from any *innovation.* Befides, one principal ufe of an univerfity education would be loft; which is, to infpire our ingenuous youth with a due veneration for

the

the founders of colleges, who framed both the ſtatute and the oath. By this means, the ſtudents are alſo early acquainted with the refinements of logick, and the ſubtilty of moral diſtinctions, and rendered leſs ſcrupulous on trivial points, which might otherwiſe impede their progreſſive fortunes in life.

Thus, Sir, animated with the moſt ardent zeal for the proſperity and glory of Britain, I have exerted my utmoſt efforts to inſpire my countrymen with a true ſpirit of obedience, ſubmiſſion, and loyalty. The church is in danger; the conſtitution is menaced; a puritanical ſavageneſs of manners ſpreads among the people; the deſponding ſeriouſneſs of fanaticiſm has contaminated their hearts and infected the land. Atheiſm and democracy have formed a new family-compact, and this new and formidable alliance will be our ruin: I ſee nothing but clouds and darkneſs in the air; for Deſpotiſm has almoſt finiſhed his ſplendid courſe, and ſcarce

emits

emits one refracted ray, to cheer the impending gloom, and prolong the twilight of his reign.

Liberty, as every true Englishman knows, can only appear " profuse of blifs and pregnant with delight," feated on her throne, with the crown and mitre in conjunction on her head, adorned in the fumptuous robes of the peerage, with the teft act in one hand, and the excife laws in the other. You will tell me, perhaps, with republican enthufiafm, that you can admire her dreffed up in ruftick fimplicity, amidft the bleak mountains of Switzerland, furrounded by a hardy peafantry of foldiers, fertilizing the rocks, and turning the very ftones into bread. You will tell me, that you can admire her in *naked majefty*, roving amidft the boundlefs forefts of America, diffufing her own fpirit of attraction through diftant regions, and uniting them by its divine energy; where confcience is not fhackled by bigotry; where

toleration

toleration is proscribed, as only implying a suspension of persecution; where obedience to the laws is the test of allegiance, and the *virtue* * of the man does not stigmatize the citizen. You will tell me, that you can admire this favourite goddess of your's, where she reduces all ranks, and levels all invidious distinctions, by restoring man to his natural equality, dignified alone by those superior talents bestowed on him by the Divinity; where all the brilliant traits of the human mind, unsubdued by the uniform glare and wide effulgence of monarchy, are displayed in their true and original colours.

I know you will tell me, that your eye is not microscopic enough to discern the minute spots in the sun of liberty that has lately risen in France; which has deigned to revisit the deserted shores of Corsica, and, in its glorious progress, has illumined the whole political atmosphere of Europe,

* See note, page 70.

M   But

But, Sir, I fit down contented, and fhall
enjoy the confcious fatisfaction of having
performed my duty.—I have painted the calamities of France; I have forewarned Britain of her danger. The fceptre trembles
in the hands of kings; the ftability of every
throne is fhaken, by the late political con-
vulfion; the fhock is not confined to France;
it acts like " the electrical returning ftroke,
which often produces fatal effects at a vaft
diftance from the place where the lightning
falls *."

I hope, Sir, you will excufe the freedom
with which I have thus publickly addreffed
you; and be perfuaded, that I can admire
the celebrated philofopher in Doctor Prieft-
ley, though I have the misfortune to differ
with him fo effentially on religion and po-
litics.

I am, Sir, Your's, &c.

J. C.

Bryanftone-ftreet,
April 26th, 1790.

* *Principles of Electricity,* by Lord Mahon, 1779.

NOTES.

N O T E S,

P. 4. (a) DR. Lowth.—" Num verendum erat he quis tyrannidem Pififtratidarum Athenis inftaurare auderet, ubi in omnibus conviviis, et æque ab infima plebe in compitis, quotidie cantitaretur Σκολιόν illud Calliftrati nefcio cujus, fed ingeniofi certe poetæ, et valde boni civis?

" Quod fi poft idus illas martias e Tyrannoctonis quifpiam tale aliquod carmen plebi tradidiffet, inque Suburram, et fori circulos, et in ora vulgi intuliffet, actum profecto fuiffet de partibus deque dominatione Cæfarum: plus mehercule valulffet unum Harmodii μελος quam Ciceronis Philippicæ omnes." Prælectiones Hebraicæ, p. 15.

It has been thus elegantly tranflated by Sir William Jones.

Verdant myrtles branchy pride,
  Shall my thirfty blade entwine:
Such HERMODIUS deck'd thy fide,
  Such ARISTOGITON thine.

Nobleft Youths! in iflands bleft,
  Not like recreant idlers dead;
You with fleet PELIDES reft,
  And with Godlike DIOMED.

Myrtle fhall our brows entwine
  While the Mufe your fame fhall tell;
'Twas at Pallas' facred fhrine,
  At your feet the Tyrant fell.

Then in Athens all was peace,
  Equal laws and liberty:
Nurfe of arts and eye of Greece;
  People valiant, firm and free!

P. 5. (*b*) The late Lord Chatham probably alluded to thé abfolution in the Vifitation of the fick, where the prieft exprefsly fays, " From the authority committed to me, I abfolve thee from all thy fins."

P. 5. (*c*) " The famous controverfy concerning the decrees of God, with refpect to the eternal condition of man, which was fet on foot by CALVIN, becomes an inexhauftible fource of intricate refearches, and abftrufe, fubtle, and inexplicable queftions. He maintained that the everlafting condition of man in a future world was determined from all eternity by the unchangeable order of the Deity ; and that this *abfolute* determination of his will and *good plea-fure*, was the *only* fource of happinefs or mifery to every individual. This opinion was in a very fhort time propagated through all the reformed churches, and in *fome places* was inferted in the national creeds and confeffions, and fo thus made a publick *article of faith*." Mofheim, vol. iv, p. 73. See alfo the 17th Article of Religion, on " Predeftination and Election."

P. 5. (*d*) " In the 17th century James Arminius, profeffor of divinity in the Univerfity of Leyden, rejected the doctrine of the church of Geneva, in relation to the deep and intricate parts of predeftination and grace ; and maintained, with the Lutherans, that God has excluded *none* from falvation by an abfolute and eternal decree. In England the fate of religion changed confiderably ; and this change, which was entirely in favour of *Arminianifm*, was principally effected by the counfels and influence of WILLIAM LAUD, Archbifhop of *Canterbury*." Mofheim, vol. iv. p. 499.

P. 5. (*e*) " Of the countries bordering on the Gold Coaft, the kingdom of Dahomey is the largeft, governed by the

the moſt abſolute tyrant that exiſts on earth. Whydah, where the Engliſh, French, and Portugueſe have forts, is a province belonging to this monarch, having been conquered by his grandfather about ſixty years ago. In Dahomey ' there is no. individual freeman, except the king. The king is abſolute maſter of the lives and properties. of his ſubjects, and he ſports with their lives in the moſt wanton and ſavage manner. Mr. Norris has ſeen at the gates of his palace two piles of heads, like ſhot in an arſenal; within the palace, the heads of perſons newly put to death are ſtrewed at the diſtance of a few yards in the paſſage that leads to the apartment of this tyrant, in order to inſpire the perſon who is to be admitted to an audience, with awe and terror. Mr. Norris does not ſpeak of one particular tyrant; it is the cuſtom of the country on great occaſions, ſuch as the reception of meſſengers from neighbouring ſtates, or of white merchants, and in general, on days of ceremonial; but the great carnage is once a year, when the poll-tax is paid by his ſubjects. Mr. Norris cannot exactly ſay how many are executed in this manner in the courſe of the year, but ſpeaks within compaſs when he reckons them at a thouſand. This is the cuſtom of the monarchy, and this power extends over his whole dominions. The kingdom is very populous, and runs about 350 miles inland. The roof of the palace is decorated with a prodigious number of human heads; and when the king means to make war, it is an expreſſion in uſe to ſay, *the palace wants thatching.* The great men of the country cut off a few heads in theſe feſtivals, which is a part only of the ſame ceremonial, and the victims are taken from thoſe deſtined for execution by the king. Parents have no ſort of property in their children in the Dahoman territories; the children belong

4   long

long entirely to the king, and are taken by his order from
their mothers at an early age, and diftributed in vil-
lages remote from the palace of their nativity, where
there is but little chance of their being feen, or at leaft
recognized by their parents afterwards. Notwithftanding
this, the people of Dahomey never quit the country; with
an extraordinary fubmiffion they revere the name of their
Sovereign, and never mention it in their moft private apartments without kneeling; fuch is the force of Education and
babit."—Reports on the Slave Trade Part the firft. Report
of the Lords of the Committee of Council of the Slave
Trade, Part IV.

P.6. (*f*) " If maidens are ravifh'd, it is their own choice,
    " Why are they fo wilful to ftruggle with men?
    " If they would but lie quiet, and ftifle their voice,
    " No devil or dean could ravifh them then."

SWIFT'S BALLAD ON AN ENGLISH DEAN.

P. 7. (*g*) So religioufly fcrupulous were the Gentiles on
this point, that, as the learned Dr. *Comber*, in his *Hiftorical Vindication of the Divine Right of Tythes*, juftly remarks,
" Melchefidec was both a prince and a prieft among
the Phœnicians, and ufed to receive tythes: fo that we
may be fure tything was very ancient there; for the
Carthaginians, who were a colony of Phœnicians, tranf-
planted into Africa, about 900 years after the death of
Sem, A. M. 3075, brought with them this cuftom from
Tyre; to which city they ufed to fend their tythe, by
one clothed in purple and prieftly robes (*a*). And Dio-
dorus Siculus more fully faith, that being in great ftraits
in their wars, they feared Hercules of Tyre was angry
with them, in that, being defcended thence, they had
ufed

ufed in the times before to fend to that god the tythe of
all their profits, but becoming rich, they neglected this,
till their mifery made them repent and fend it as before (b).—Mr. Selden grants that the Grecians confe-
crated their tythes fo often to Apollo, that he was called
Δεκατηφορ℘, which may be tranflated the Tythetaker.—
The hymn he cites out of Callimachus, page 30, fhews,
that firft fruits, in the proportion of a tenth, were every
year fent to Delos, unto the fame God; but Mr. S. hath
omitted the two next verfes, which exprefsly fay, " thefe
were the tythes of corn." And we may well fuppofe he
had tythes of all profits, when fo infamous a gain as that
of Rhodope afforded a confecration to him (c): and that
this was ufual, may be gathered from that other courtezan, in the old poem, " who vows to offer the tenth
of all her gains to Venus" (d).—The Siphnians paid a
yearly tythe of their mines (e); and it was doubtlefs paid
as a due; becaufe upon their omitting it, they loft their
mines, by the juftice of the gods.—Porphyry alfo relates,
out of Hefiod, one of the oldeft poets, that the gods had
utterly deftroyed an atheiftical and irreligious people,
called Theos, becaufe they paid no firft fruits, as they
ought to have done (f): which divine judgement muft
have been long before Hefiod's time; and, even then,
it feems it was fo unufual an impiety, that the deftruction of that people was believed to proceed from that
caufe. Yet judgements are not wont to be fent down
upon whole nations for omitting arbitrary and accidental
acts of extraordinary devotion."

Hift. Vindication, &c. p. 29, 30, 34.

(a) Juftin. Hiftor. l. 18, p. 186.   (b) Diodor. Sic. Hiftor. l. 5.
(c) Herodot. Euterp. l. 2, p. 160. , (d) Antholog. l. 6.
(e) Herodot. l. 3, p. 210. (f) Porphyr. de Abftin. l. 4, f. 8, p. 56.

A few

A few of the *rabbis*, of the fect of the Sadducees, have aſſerted, that tythes were paid to the Jewiſh prieſts, (the tribe of Levi,) as a compenſation for their giving up their ſhare in the diviſion of the land of Canaan, to which they were equally entitled, as one of the twelve tribes of Iſrael ;—but this opinion has juſtly been deemed heretical, and is clearly proved ſo, by the learned and orthodox Dr. Comber.

What an amiable trait does this learned divine give of the pious conduct of Rhodope! but why ſhe dedicated the tythe of her amorous gain to Apollo, the doctor has not explained : Venus, under whoſe propitious banners ſhe ſerved, might have received the gift with more propriety. To her we find the other courtezan alluded to by this reverend writer, made her votive offerings. The epigram in the *Anthologia* to which he refers, may be thus freely tranſlated :

Fair Nicarete long to Pallas bows,
To Venus now ſhe breathes her fervent vows:
Adieu, ſhe cries, my diſtaff, and my loom,
The houſewife's taſk no more ſhall waſte my bloom ;
Such taſks the old and ugly may employ,
While feſtive love ſhall thrill my ſoul with joy.
With roſes crown'd, and fluſh'd with warm deſire,
To Cytherea ſtill I'll tune my lyre :
Speed thou my gain, my native charm refine !
A tythe I'll give, 'tis your's by right divine.

　　　　　　　　　Anthol. lib. vi. c. 8. ep. 9.

I am told a clauſe was to have been inſerted in a bill, intended to have been brought in by a worthy Baronet, for the regulation and reformation of women of the town, obliging them to pay a *tenth*, for the augmentation of thoſe curates' ſalaries who have not above

　　　　　　　　　　　　　　　　twenty

twenty pounds a year;—no doubt with the unanimous approbation of the bench of bifhops.

P. 9. (*h*) " The tythe, and every other land tax of this kind, under the appearance of perfect equality, are very unequal taxes; a certain portion of the produce being, in different fituations, equivalent to a very different portion of the rent. In fome very rich lands, the produce is fo great, that the one-half of it is fully fufficient to replace to the farmer his capital employed in cultivation, together with the ordinary profits of farming ftock in the neighbourhood; the other half, or, what comes to the fame thing, the value of the other half, he could afford to pay as rent to the landlord, if there was no tythe:—but if the tenth of the profit is taken from him by way of tythe, he muft require an abatement of the fifth part of his rent, otherwife he cannot get back his capital with the ordinary profit. In this cafe, the rent of the landlord, inftead of amounting to a half, or five-tenths of the whole produce, will amount only to four-tenths of it. In poorer lands, on the contrary, the produce is fometimes fo fmall, and the expence of cultivation fo great, that it requires four-fifths of the whole produce to replace to the farmer his capital with the ordinary profit. In this cafe, though there was no tythe, the rent of the landlord could amount to no more than one-fifth or two-tenths of the whole produce. But if the farmer pays one-tenth of the produce in the way of tythe, he muft require an equal abatement of the rent of the landlord, which will thus be reduced to one tenth only of the whole produce. Upon the rent of rich lands, the tythe may fometimes be a tax of no more than one-fifth part, or four fhillings in the pound; whereas upon that of

N

poorer

poorer lands it may fometimes be a tax of one-half, or of ten fhillings in the pound.

" The tythe, as it is frequently a very unequal tax upon the rent, fo it is always a great difcouragement both to the improvements of the landlord and to the cultivation of the farmer: the one cannot venture to make the moft important, which are generally the moft expenfive, improvements; nor the other to raife the moft valuable, which are generally too the moft expenfive, crops, when the church, which lays out no part of the exprnce, is to fhare fo very largely in the profit. The cultivation of madder was for a long time confined by the tythe to the. United Provinces; which, being Prefbyterian countries, and, upon that account, exempted from this deftructive-tax, enjoyed a fort of monopoly of that ufeful dying drug, againft the reft of Europe. The late attempts to introduce the culture of this plant into England, have been made only in confequence of the ftatute which enacted that five fhillings an acre fhould be received in lieu of all manner of tythe upon madder." Smith's Wealth of Nations, Vol. III.

P. 11. *(i)* " The *Bifhops* affumed, in many places, a princely authority, particularly thofe who had the greateft number of churches under their infpection, and who prefided over the moft opulent affemblies. They appropriated to their evangelical function the fplendid enfigns, of temporal majefty.

" A throne, furrounded with minifters, exalted above his equals the fervant of the meek and humble Jefus; and fumptuous garments dazzled the eyes and minds of the multitude into an ignorant veneration for their arrogated authority. The example of the Bifhops was ambitioufly imitated by the *Prefbyters,* who, neglecting the

facred

facred duties of their flations, abandoned themfelves to the indolence and delicacy of an effeminate and luxurious life. The *Deacons*, beholding the Prefbyters deferting thus their functions, boldly ufurped their rights and privileges; and the effects of a corrupt ambition were fpread through every rank of the facred order." Mofheim's Ecclefiaftical Hiftory, vol. 1. p. 216.

P. 14. (*k*) Thefe apoftates would fain revive Cato's ftoical creed, preferved by Lucan, Book IX. ver. 576,

Hæremus cuncti fupcris, templòque tacente
Nil facimus non fponte dei : nec vocibus ullis
Numen eget : dixitque femel nafcentibus auctor,
Quidquid fcire licet: fterileis nec legit arenas
Ut caneret paucis, merfitque hôc pulvere verum.
Eftne dei fedes nifi terra, & pontus & aër,
Et cœlum & virtus? Superos quid quærimus ultrà?
Jupiter eft, quodcunque vides, quocunque moveris.

P. 17. (*l*) The work is entitled ' A Plan of Lectures on the Principles of Non-Conformity, for the Inftruction of Catechumens;' by R. Robinfon. It made its firft appearance about the year 1778. In the year 1781 it had ran through four editions, and a *fifth* was fent *abroad*. This rapid fale is no lefs than the folemn judgement of the eaftern affociation, and a proof of the approbation with which it has been received by the general body of the non-conformifts." Review of the Cafe of the Proteftant Diffenters, page 23.

P. 17. (*m*) All thefe fchifmatick ideas are confonant to thofe of Mofheim, whofe character and writings I have already defcribed.

 " Neither Chrift himfelf, nor his holy apoftles, have commanded any thing clearly or exprefsly concerning

the

the external form of the church, and the precife method according to which it fhould be governed. From this we may infer, that the regulation of this was, in fome meafure, to be accommodated to the time.

"The people were undoubtedly the firft in authority; for the apoftles fhewed, by their own example, that nothing of moment was to be carried on or determined without the confent of the affembly (a): and fuch a method of proceeding was both prudent and neceffary in thofe critical times. It was afterwards judged neceffary that one man of diftinguifhed gravity and wifdom fhould prefide in the council of Prefbyters, in order to diftribute among his colleagues their feveral tafks, and to be a centre of union to the whole fociety. This perfon was at firft ftyled the *angel* (b) of the church to which he belonged, but was afterwards diftinguifhed by the name of *bifhop*, or infpector; a name borrowed from the Greek language, Επισκοπθ-, infpector, and expreffing the principal part of the epifcopal function, which was to infpect into, and fuperintend the affairs of the church." Mofheim, vol. 1, cent. 1.

P. 20. (n) "Marriage was permitted to all the various ranks and orders of the clergy, high and low. Thofe, however, who continued in a ftate of celibacy, obtained by this abftinence a higher reputation of fanctity and value than others. This was owing to an almoft general perfuafion, that they who took wives were of all others the moft fubject to the power of malignant demons; and as it was of infinite importance to the interefts of the church that no impure or malevolent fpirit entered into the bodies of fuch as were appointed to govern or inftruct others, fo the people were defirous that the clergy fhould ufe their

(a) Acts, i. 15. vi. 3. xv. 4. xxi. 22. (b) Rev. ii. 3.

utmoft

utmoſt efforts to abſtain from the pleaſures of conjugal life. Many of the ſacred orders, eſpecially in *Africa*, conſented to ſatisfy the deſires of the people; and endeavoured to do this in ſuch a manner as not to offer an entire violence to their own inclinations. For this purpoſe, they formed connections with thoſe women who had made vows of perpetual chaſtity; and it was an ordinary thing for an eccleſiaſtick to admit one of theſe ſaints to a participation of his bed; but ſtill under the moſt ſolemn declarations, that nothing paſſed in this commerce contrary to the rules of chaſtity and virtue. Theſe holy concubines were called by the Greeks Γυνεισακτοι, and by the Latins, Mulieres Superinductæ."

Moſheim, vol. 1, p. 218.

P. 22. (*o*) " Je reprends la ſuite de mes réflexions, et je place ici une obſervation importante ; c'eſt que plus l'étendue des impôts entretient le peuple dans l'abattement et dans la miſère, plus il eſt indiſpenſable de lui donner une éducation religieuſe, car c'eſt dans l'irritation du malheur, qu'on a ſur tout beſoin, et d'une chaîne puiſſante, et d'une conſolation journalière. Les abus ſucceſſifs de la force et de l'autorité, en bouleverſant tous les rapports qui exiſtoient originairement entre les hommes, ont élevé, au milieu d'eux, un édifice tellement artificiel, et où il règne tant de diſproportion, que l'idée d'un dieu y eſt devenue plus néceſſaire que jamais, pour ſervir de nivellement à cet aſſemblage confus de diſparitès de tout genre." De l'Importance des Opinions Religieuſes ; par M. Necker, p. 18.

P. 29. (*p*) I am aware that Monſieur Gebelin in his *Monde Primitive*, maintains another hypotheſis, with great ingenuity, founded on his aſtoniſhing knowledge in etymology,

is fuppofed to difhonour whoever is fubject to it, and to degrade him below not only the rank of a gentleman, but that of a burgher; and whoever rents the lands of another, becomes fubject to it. No gentleman, nor even a burgher, who has ftock, will fubmit to this degradation. This tax therefore not only hinders the ftock which accumulates upon the land from being employed in its improvement, but drives away all other ftock from it. The ancient tenths and fifteenths, fo ufual in England in former times, feem, fo far as they affected the land, to have been taxes of the fame nature with the taille." Smith's Wealth of Nations, vol. 2, p. 96.

P. 56 (*s*) " Yet though the reftoration of ancient theology is the object of the moft ardent defires, I much fear that a period ftill more barbarous, with refpect to philofophy, that an age ftill darker and more debafed, muft precede its eftablifhment on the earth. Prodigies and deftruction attended, as we fhall obferve in the enfuing hiftory, its departure from mankind; and defolation will doubtlefs be the harbinger of its future appearance.

" The orb of viciffitude produces renovation and decay, in regular fucceffion, and marks, as it revolves, the dormant events of future periods with the *ruinous* characters of the paft. Let us therefore patiently wait for, and joyfully expect, the happy moment when the breezes of philofophy fhall arife with abundance and vigour, and impel the veffel of theology, laden with the riches of wifdom, on our natal coaft.

" The revolution is certain, however remote ; and the profpect is of itfelf fufficient to increafe the vigour of exertion, and animate the expectations of hope; to enable us to brave the ftorms of ecclefiaftical perfecution, and vanquifh the refiftance of folly."

Taylor's Preface to the *Commentaries of Proclus*.

F I N I S.

B

www.ingramcontent.com/pod-product-compliance
Lightning Source LLC
Chambersburg PA
CBHW031438270326
41930CB00007B/774